29817

D1580401

HEINEMANN HISTORY

THE ITALIAN RENAISSANCE

STUDY UNITS

Peter Mantin

Heinemann Library,
an imprint of Heinemann Publishers (Oxford) Ltd,
Halley Court, Jordan Hill, Oxford OX2 8EJ

OXFORD LONDON EDINBURGH MADRID
ATHENS BOLOGNA PARIS MELBOURNE
SYDNEY AUCKLAND SINGAPORE TOKYO
IBADAN NAIROBI HARARE GABORONE
PORTSMOUTH NH (USA)

This edition first published 1994

**British Library Cataloguing in Publication Data is available
from the British Library on request.**

ISBN 0–431–07352–X

Designed by Ron Kamen, Green Door Design Ltd, Basingstoke

Illustrated by Jeff Edwards and Sharon Lunn

Printed in China

The cover shows *The Journey of the Magi*, by Benozzo Gozzoli.
It was commissioned by Piero de' Medici and is painted on the
chapel walls of the Medici Palace in Florence.

Acknowledgements

The author and publisher would like to thank the following for
permission to reproduce photographs:

Bodleian Library: 1.1B
Oswaldo Böhm: 6.2
Bridgeman Art Library: Cover, 2.4A, 3.1B, 3.2A, 4.3F, 5.3A
Fotomass Index: 5.4B
Girandon/Alinari: 2.6
Girandon/Musée Condé de Chantilly: 4.1F
Reproduced by courtesy of the Trustees, the National Gallery,
London: 3.4B, 6.3E
Pierpont Morgan Library, New York: 3.4A
Scala: 1.1A, 2.2E, 2.3B, 2.3C, 2.3G, 2.5B, 3.1A, 3.3A, 4.1G,
4.1H, 4.1I, 4.2C, 4.3A, 5.3B, 5.3F, 6.1B, 6.1C, 6.1D
Ronald Sheridan: 4.1A, 4.1B, 4.1C, 4.1D, 6.3C
Staatliche Museum, Berlin: 5.1B
Trinity College, Cambridge: 5.1A
Windsor Castle, Royal Library © 1991, Her Majesty the
Queen: 1.1C
Woodmansterne Picture Library: 6.3F
Woodmansterne Picture Library/PNS: 4.1E

We would also like to thank the following for permission to
use copyright material:

Grisewood & Dempsey Ltd for Source 4.2D which is taken
from *The Roman World* by Mike Corbishley, Kingfisher Books,
1986; Scientific American for Source 4.3B which is taken from
Scientific American, January 1991.

Thanks are also due to Russell Price of the University of
Lancaster and Andy Harmsworth of the Simon Langton Girls
School for their invaluable comments on the original
manuscript.

Details of written sources
In some sources the wording or sentence structure has been
simplified to ensure that the source is accessible.

Geoffrey Barraclough, *The Times Atlas of World History*, Book
Club Associates, 1978: 2.1B
Alison Brown, *The Renaissance*, Longman, 1988: 2.1A, 2.2A,
2.2B, 2.2C, 2.3D, 2.4B, 4.3D
Peter Burke, *The Renaissance*, Macmillan, 1987: 4.2A
Ritchie Calder, *Leonardo*, Heinemann, 1970: 3.3B, 4.3C
Kenneth Clark, *Civilization*, BBC Books, 1969: 3.2C, 5.1C,
6.3D
Mike Corbishley, *The Roman World*, Kingfisher, 4.2B
Vincent Cronin, *The Florentine Renaissance*, Fontana, 1967:
2.3H, 5.4D
T. Dowley, *The History of Christianity*, Lion, 1977: 5.4A
E. Eisenstein, *The Printing Revolution in Early Modern Europe*,
CUP, 1983: 5.1D
E. H. Gombrick, *The Story of Art*, Phaidon, 1972: 3.2D
D. Hay, *The Age of the Renaissance*, Book Club Associates,
1986: 6.2B
H. Janson, *The History of Art*, Prentice–Hall, 1969: 3.2B
R. Lopez, *The Economy 1350–1500*, Wiley, 1953: 6.2A
Edward MacCurdy, *The Notebooks of Leonardo da Vinci*, Tudor,
1948: 5.3C, 5.3E
Niccolò Machiavelli, *The Prince*, Penguin Classics, 1970:
2.6A, 2.6C, 2.6D, 2.6E, 2.6F, 2.6G, 2.6H
Peter Murray, *The Architecture of the Italian Renaissance*,
Thames and Hudson, 1981: 2.3A
J. New, *The Renaissance and Reformation*, Wiley, 1977: 5.1E
G. Parker, *The Military Revolution*, CUP, 1978: 5.2B
J. H. Plumb (Ed.), *The Penguin Book of the Renaissance*,
Penguin Books Ltd, 1964: 2.3F
J. H. Plumb (Ed.), *The Renaissance*, Horizon Magazine, NY,
1961: 2.4C, 2.4D, 2.4E, 2.6B, 5.4C
Joe Scott, *Medicine Through Time*, Holmes McDougall, 1988:
5.5E, 5.5F
D. M. Smith, *The Images of Man: Frederigo da Montelfetro*,
Horizon, 1961: 6.3A
E. Wright, *The Medieval and Renaissance World*, Hamlyn, 1969:
2.2D

CONTENTS

1.1 The Man who Cut Up Bodies

The crowd groaned with horror as the hangman did his job. The body of the criminal swung lifelessly from the rope. Soon the crowd began to lose interest and drift away. After a while there was only one man left watching the dead body sway in the wind. This man was doing a very careful drawing of the corpse. At last the body was taken down and brought to a place where very few people dared to visit – the city morgue.

The morgue was a dark, lonely place. You may imagine what the smell of the rotting bodies was like if you remember that 500 years ago there were no fridges – and that dead bodies rot very quickly, especially in hot countries like Italy. The artist usually worked alone in the middle of the night. He had his own oil lamp so that he could see the parts of the body he was going to cut up and draw. It was a race against time. Sometimes he even took pieces of the body home with him so he could finish the drawing before the flesh had gone completely bad.

A

A drawing of a hanged man from the notebooks of Leonardo da Vinci, written in about 1510.

B

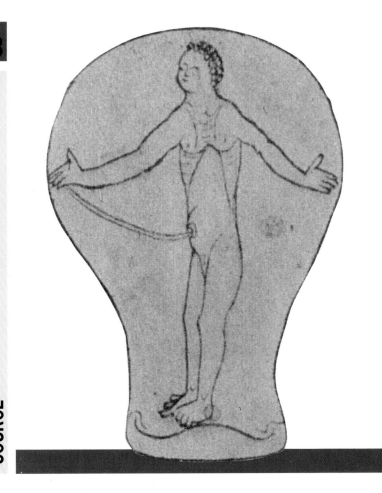

Drawing of a foetus inside its mother from a medieval textbook about the work of a midwife.

The man who had done the drawings in the morgue and at the gallows was **Leonardo da Vinci**. He also did the drawing seen in Source C. Leonardo's notebooks tell us about the way he worked. He said that if you want to know about the parts of the body you must cut up bodies and examine them carefully. Only in this way will you learn about the body.

Leonardo lived at a time when all sorts of **changes** were taking place. Some of these changes began in Italy, the centre of the Roman Catholic religion in Europe. Between the 14th and 16th centuries, people began to look at the world in a different way. The ideas and knowledge of the Greeks and Romans had been lost during the Middle Ages. In sculpture, painting and architecture, these ideas were now being re-discovered. Historians have used the word **Renaissance** to describe this period of time. It means 'rebirth'. This book tells the story of some of these important changes.

Ludovico Sforza

Ludovico Sforza (1452–1508) was the ruler of Milan who employed Leonardo da Vinci, as much for his military and mechanical ideas as for his art. Ludovico became Duke of Milan in 1494, after a long power struggle while his nephew was supposedly Duke. In 1499 the French invaded. Ludovico was overthrown. He was taken to France where he died in 1508 in a windowless, underground prison cell.

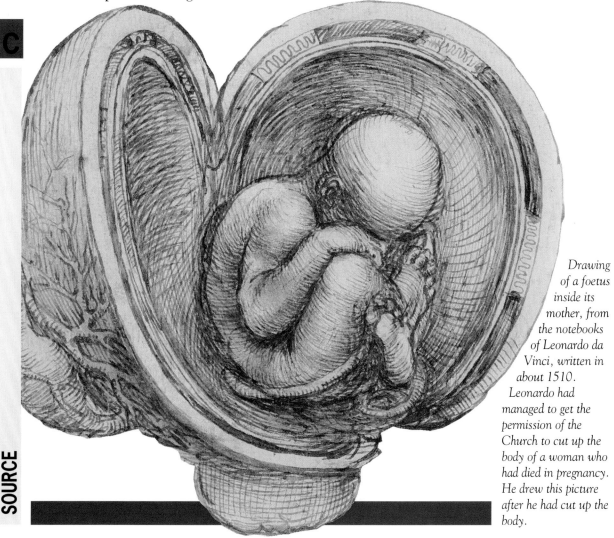

C

SOURCE

Drawing of a foetus inside its mother, from the notebooks of Leonardo da Vinci, written in about 1510. Leonardo had managed to get the permission of the Church to cut up the body of a woman who had died in pregnancy. He drew this picture after he had cut up the body.

2.1 City-States

In about 1400 most of Europe was ruled by kings and princes, helped by nobles and churchmen. The head of the Church was the **Pope**. He claimed that he was descended from St Peter and that he spoke God's word to the people. He told people all over Europe how to behave and what to believe in. He ruled the **Papal States** – an important part of Italy.

At this time many more people had learned to read and write. Universities were being set up in a number of European cities. The Church played an important part in setting up universities. Islamic science and technology had found its way to Europe through trading and other contacts. Islamic scholars had translated important books by ancient Greek and Roman writers. In 1453 the Islamic Turks captured Constantinople, the capital of what had been the eastern Roman Empire. Many people fled to Italy. Among the things which were brought to Italy were books written by ancient Greeks and Romans.

Why should important changes have been taking place in Italy at this time, rather than anywhere else? If you look at the map you will see that parts of Italy were run in a different way from the rest of Europe. Italy was not a 'nation-state' in the way we know it today. It was made up of a number of **city-states**. The ancient Greeks had settled in southern Italy and had brought with them the idea of the city-state – a city which governs itself. The Romans had conquered the Greeks, but copied some of their best ideas. If the word 'civilization' means the art of living in cities, then you could call the ancient Greeks and Romans civilized. One thousand years after the fall of the Roman Empire there were still many places which had kept Latin writing and Roman laws. Roman buildings, roads and statues could be found in many Italian cities. People felt a great pride in the achievements of ancient Roman writers, generals, emperors, sculptors, artists and builders.

Italian cities played an important part in the **trade** of Europe. **Florence** was an important centre of industry, trade and banking. **Venice** was an important place on a number of trade routes. Spices, silk and cotton came to Venice from Asia.

From 'The Times-Atlas of World History' by G. Barraclough, 1979. The figures are based on the reports of traders who came to and from Venice in the early 15th century.

B **SOURCE**

Destination	Journey time from Venice in days
London	27
Damascus	80
Alexandria	65
Palermo	22
Lisbon	46
Nuremberg	20
Valladolid	29
Lyons	12
Naples	9
Brussels	16

Gold and ivory were brought by Arabs from Africa. Galleys sailed from Venice to ports all over Europe. The money for some of these voyages was raised in Venice. Merchants from Venice travelled north to do business at Bruges, the centre of the cloth trade. Venice, Naples and Milan all had populations of over 100,000 people by about the year 1500. Of the northern European cities only Paris had such a large population.

Europe in the early 15th century. The borders of the Italian city-states changed frequently because there were often quarrels between them.

Doge Francesco Foscari

Francesco Foscari (1373–1457) became Doge of Venice in 1423. Venice was one of many city-states in Italy at the time, all fighting each other. The Doge was the elected head of the state of Venice. He was a controversial and ambitious man. His reign, the longest in Venetian history, saw much fighting and much creative work. Great palaces were built along the canals of Venice and the Rialto bridge was rebuilt. Artists worked on public buildings and there were spectacular pageants and shows for important visitors. Venice also went to war with other Italian states and the Turks. The fighting went on for thirty years and was expensive but Venice did expand. It lost land to the Turks, however. Foscari had many enemies. His son was accused of treason and exiled. Foscari was accused of murder, and forced to resign. He died eight days later.

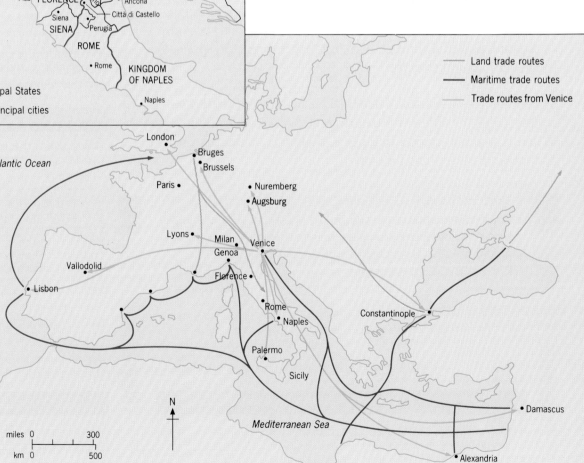

2.2 Florence

In the 15th century many important changes were taking place in Florence, an Italian city. What sort of a place was Florence?

Florence was a rich city in the early 15th century. The silk, cotton and wool **industries** made some people in Florence very wealthy. Industries like these were organized into **guilds**. Guilds were organized groups of people involved in the same craft or trade. They were set up to protect their members' interests and wanted the best of everything for themselves and their city.

Trade had made Florence rich. All sorts of goods were traded with many distant lands. Some traders also got rich by lending money and making the borrowers pay interest. This way of making money was not allowed by the Church, but we know it happened. Some moneylenders paid for the building of churches out of their profits.

Florence was also a very important **banking** centre. Rich bankers lent money to powerful people like popes and kings. Princes from all over Europe looked to the bankers of Florence to raise money to pay for wars. One family, the **Medici**, became so rich and powerful through banking that it took over some of the government of the city.

Many rich people became **patrons**. This meant that they gave **commissions** (or orders) for paintings and other works of art. When Florence became a rich place, there were more patrons and more artists looking for work.

There is not enough good farming land around Florence to feed the rising population of the city. So the people go abroad to make their fortune before returning to Florence. Travelling through other countries they have seen the way other people live and have taken the best ideas. Whoever is not a merchant, and has not seen foreign countries and brought things back from abroad, is thought to be nothing.

From 'History of Florence' by Gregorio Dati. Dati was a merchant who also wrote books in the 15th century.

The Medici and other bankers used their agents in Bruges to send Greek and Roman books, as well as French paintings and tapestries, to Italy. In return they sent works of art from Florence to Bruges. So trade was important. New ideas from Florence were exchanged for northern works of art.

An explanation of how trade affected art, from 'The Renaissance' by Alison Brown, 1988.

I have also spent a lot of money on my house and on the church of Santa Maria Novella. All of these things give me the greatest pleasure, because they serve the honour of God as well as the city, and they make sure I am remembered.

The merchant Giovanni Rucellai explains why he paid for the building of a church, 1473.

During this period Florence was the centre of the European banking system. The Medici had branches at Milan, Naples, Pisa and Venice in Italy, at Geneva, Lyons and Avignon in central Europe, and at Bruges and London in the north. They played an important part in European trade.

From 'The Medieval and Renaissance World', by E. Wright, 1969.

Florence in about 1490.

Giovanni di Bicci de' Medici

Giovanni de' Medici (1360–1429) was one of the Medici family who ruled the city-state of Florence from 1434–1737 with only two short breaks from power. Giovanni was the first of the Medici to make a lot of money and gain power in the city. He did not start life as a rich man, but he soon made a fortune from his banking business. Rich merchants, especially bankers, were expected to help to run the city-states and Giovanni did just this, holding several government jobs. He set up banks in other city-states too, most profitably in Rome, where he lent money to Pope John XXIII. Like other rich men at the time, Giovanni spent a lot of his money on the arts, both for himself and for the city of Florence.

2.3 Cosimo de' Medici

We have seen that rich patrons from Florence bought work from artists. One of the most famous of these patrons was **Cosimo de' Medici**. His family ran an important and successful bank which was powerful in many parts of Europe.

The Library at the monastery of San Marco, Florence. Cosimo ordered it to be built to store the precious Greek, Islamic and Roman books which were being found and translated. Scholars came from far and wide to work at this library.

Cosimo put his friends and members of his family into important jobs in the guilds. His other main weapon was just as clever. It soon became clear that your tax bill varied according to whether you supported Cosimo or not. Unlike so many other 15th century politicians, Cosimo probably never murdered anybody. He found it worked just as well to make his enemies bankrupt.

From 'The Architecture of the Italian Renaissance' by Peter Murray, 1981.

C SOURCE

Vespaciano

Vespaciano (1421–98) was a bookseller in Florence. He was a friend of Cosimo de' Medici and wrote admiring accounts of Cosimo's life. Vespaciano was buried near Cosimo in the church of Santa Croce.

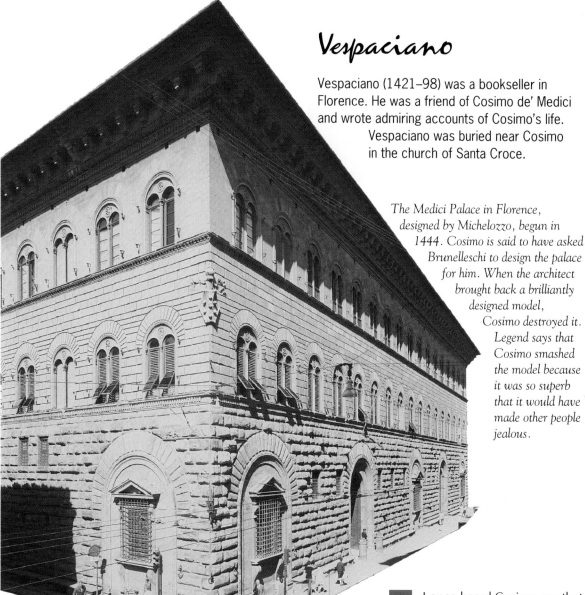

The Medici Palace in Florence, designed by Michelozzo, begun in 1444. Cosimo is said to have asked Brunelleschi to design the palace for him. When the architect brought back a brilliantly designed model, Cosimo destroyed it. Legend says that Cosimo smashed the model because it was so superb that it would have made other people jealous.

D SOURCE

Cosimo knew that if he wanted God to have mercy on him and allow him to stay rich, he would have to behave in a holy way. So he remembered some money he had come by not quite cleanly. Wanting to lift this weight from his shoulders he went to talk to the Pope, who told him he should pay for a church building.

From 'The Life of Cosimo de' Medici' by Vespasiano. He lived from 1421 to 1498 and met Cosimo.

E SOURCE

I once heard Cosimo say that the great mistake of his life was that he did not begin to spend his wealth ten years earlier; because knowing the attitudes of his fellow citizens, he was sure that 50 years later no memory would remain of his personality or him or his family, except the few buildings he might have ordered to be built.

From 'Memoirs' by Vespasiano.

Cosimo was born in 1389. When he was a boy he collected coins, medals and vases. His friend Niccolò Niccoli had collected 800 books and was keen for Cosimo to use some of the family money to build a great library.

Cosimo's father, Giovanni, had been one of the most important men in Florence. He had paid for a great architect called **Brunelleschi** to build a hospital and a beautiful church. He had also angered some of the rich men of Florence by making them pay heavy taxes. Giovanni died in 1429. Cosimo took over the family business. He also became involved in politics.

In 1433 a rival family, called the **Albizzi**, managed to get Cosimo arrested as a danger to the people of Florence. His enemies said he was getting so rich and powerful that he was trying to take over. In jail Cosimo bribed people to get the charges dropped. He was set free but was ordered to leave Florence. Cosimo took his money with him and waited for his enemies to quarrel among themselves. In 1434 he came back in triumph. The Albizzi were sent away and from that moment Cosimo's power increased even more.

During the next 30 years Cosimo made his family even richer. He became the most powerful man in Florentine politics. Cosimo had the money and power of a king but he was clever enough not to call himself one. For most of that time he brought peace to Florence. He avoided wars by doing deals with nearby city-states. He was also banker to the Pope and to the government, and paid the largest tax bill in Florence. When he died in 1464 they wrote *Pater Patriae* on his tomb. It means 'Father of the Country'.

Government in Florence

The rich people of Florence were not just businessmen. They were also often involved in running the city. The people of Florence seem to have been proud to have been part of a republic. They weren't ruled by a king but by a council, made up of traders, bankers and people from the guilds. These guilds were like special clubs of people, each belonging to a certain trade or type of job. Cosimo did not rule Florence by force; he wasn't like a modern government minister either. Jobs on the Florentine council were rotated. Cosimo's most important position was as head of the Medici bank. He used the influence of the bank during the 30 years in which he was involved in the politics of Florence.

This statue of David by Donatello was ordered and paid for by Cosimo in 1439. The statue has been called a landmark in the history of civilization. It is thought to have been the first free-standing nude statue made since Roman times. Donatello had been to Rome to study ancient buildings and statues. His 'David' is thought to have been based on descriptions of ancient Greek and Roman statues.

Cosimo treated Donatello as a close personal friend. He paid him wages and in his old age gave him a pension. After a long stay in Padua, when his sculpture was praised to the skies, Donatello decided to return to Florence. He knew that if he was criticized he would produce better work. Cosimo was prepared to criticize him.

From 'The Florentine Renaissance' by Vincent Cronin, 1967.

Donatello

Donatello (1386–1466) was christened Donatto di Betto Bardi. It is thought that he had his first training in sculpture with a sculptor for Florence Cathedral. Certainly, by 1407, he was working in the shops of a bronze sculptor who worked for the Cathedral. Cosimo de' Medici took a special interest in Donatello who was more concerned with sculpting than day-to-day concerns. Donatello's marvellous statues, in both marble and bronze, make him, to many people, the founder of modern sculpture.

2.4 Magnificent Lorenzo?

Lorenzo de' Medici is often called 'Lorenzo the Magnificent' in history books. What was 'magnificent' about him?

Cosimo died in 1464. For more than 30 years he had been the most important man in Florence. His son Piero took over but lived only for another five years. So in 1469 Cosimo's grandson, the 21-year-old Lorenzo, had to take over the family bank. He chose people to manage the bank and worked with other great Florentine families to rule the city.

SOURCE

A detail from 'The Journey of the Magi' a painting ordered by the Medici. The man on the white horse is believed to be Lorenzo.

Lorenzo had enemies. The **Pazzi** family were envious of the wealth and power of the Medici. They plotted with Pope Sixtus IV to get rid of Lorenzo and his brother Giuliano. The Pope wanted more power in Italy and saw Lorenzo as a threat. At Easter in 1478, Lorenzo and Giuliano were attending Mass in Florence Cathedral. When Giuliano went forward to receive communion a Pazzi priest smashed him over the back of his head. He was then stabbed 18 times to make sure he was dead. Lorenzo was also attacked, but managed to escape with little injury. The Pazzi plot had failed. Lorenzo dealt savagely with the plotters. Some were tortured; others were executed in public.

Cosimo had tried to make sure that he wasn't seen to be getting too powerful. Lorenzo did not bother. After the Pazzi plot, Lorenzo made it clear that he was in charge.

The tyrant keeps his people busy with shows and festivals, so that they will not notice what he is really doing. Tyrants give in to praise; they do not listen to the poor and they do not criticize the rich. The people are made to pay heavy taxes. When widows come weeping they are told; go to sleep.

SOURCE

From a sermon by the preacher Savonarola in San Marco monastery, Florence, 1491. San Marco had been founded by the Medici family.

After the death of Cosimo, the Medici bank found it more difficult to be successful. Lorenzo's financial position gradually worsened. Many firms collapsed in the 1460s and Lorenzo did not have as much money to spend as his grandfather. By the 1490s the bank was in serious trouble. Lorenzo did not have the money to spend on costly wars, even if he had wanted to fight them. So he avoided wars when he could and tried to keep the peace between the different states in Italy. Many people saw him as a wise peacemaker. He was also praised for his poetry Few kings or princes have managed to be poets as well as leaders.

Lorenzo was criticized by the preacher **Savonarola**. Huge crowds came to hear Savonarola preach terrible sermons, which predicted disaster for those who lived a life of luxury and turned away from God's true message. In 1492 Lorenzo died. Two years later Italy was at war again and the Medici had been expelled from Florence.

C **SOURCE**

He wanted glory above all other men. He showed favour to poetry, music, building and painting, so that the city overflowed with all these graces. Though the city was not free under him, it would have been impossible to have found a better tyrant.

From 'Florentine Histories', composed 1508–9, by the historian Francesco Guicciardini. He was a friend of Machiavelli.

D **SOURCE**

In those peaceful days Lorenzo always kept his city feasting. All the people mourned his death. As soon as Lorenzo died all those bad seeds began to sprout. They are still ruining Italy.

From 'History of Florence' by Niccolò Machiavelli, 1525. Machiavelli was an opponent of the Medici in Florence.

E **SOURCE**

Led by Lorenzo, Florence became the cultural capital of Italy. He set the pace and other princes had to compete. He was the highest bidder for the services of artists and scholars and carried off all the prizes for the glory of Florence and the Medici family. He set up a branch of Pisa University and spared no expense to get the best teachers in Italy.

From 'Lorenzo' by Ralph Roeder, 1961.

Francesco de' Pazzi

Francesco de' Pazzi (died 1478) was a member of the Pazzi family, who were banking rivals of the Medici family. They had commissioned Brunelleschi to build a family chapel next to the famous church of Santa Croce.

In 1464, Francesco was manager of the family bank in Rome. He was described as a small, fidgety man who was arrogant and wanted to be famous. In 1478, Francesco was part of a plot to make the Pazzi rulers of Florence rather than the Medici. The plot was supported by Pope Sixtus IV.

It was planned to kill Lorenzo de' Medici and his brother, Giuliano, while they were at mass in the Cathedral on Easter Day. Guiliano was killed, but Lorenzo managed to escape. The people of Florence hunted down the Pazzi plotters and killed them. Francesco was dragged from his hiding place in his palace. He was stripped naked, a rope was tied round his neck and he was thrown out of the window to hang next to four other plotters. Among these was a priest. The situation looked bad for everyone, even Sixtus, but was eventually smoothed over. The Pazzi were not a serious threat to the Medici again.

2.5 Savonarola

Lorenzo de' Medici may have been called 'the magnificent' but that doesn't mean that he was popular with everyone. Girolamo Savonarola (1452–98) was a monk who preached sermons in which he criticized Lorenzo.

Savonarola came to the monastery of San Marco in Florence in 1491. He already had a reputation as a great preacher. Savonarola said that God had told him that a terrible dagger would be raised over the city of Florence. He warned the people that there would be an awful day of disaster for Florence. Savonarola said that the people and their leaders had turned away from the word of God and they would be punished for their sins. People flocked to hear him criticize the behaviour of the Pope and of the Medici.

A *woodcut made in the early 16th century showing Savonarola preaching against the Pope and the Medici.*

Lorenzo died in 1492. He had left instructions that if the French invaded Florence the people must stand firm and not give in. In 1494 the French King, Charles VIII, invaded northern Italy with a large army. He was intending to conquer Naples. He had to go through Tuscany on his way to Naples. Lorenzo's son Piero was not a great leader and the French invasion made him panic. Piero gave in to the French without a fight. He surrendered the important town of Pisa and three other fortresses. The people of Florence were so angry with Piero that they made him leave the city. The days of the Medici seemed to be over.

A **Great Council** was set up in Florence. It had 3,000 members who were not chosen only from the ranks of the richest people in Florence. Savonarola became involved in the political life of the city. He even went to meet Charles VIII and told the people of Florence that Charles was restoring peace and liberty to Florence and to all of Italy.

Fra Angelico

Fra Angelico (1400–55) was christened Guido di Pietro. In 1420 he became a monk in the Dominican monastery at Fiesole and did many of his paintings there. His paintings were always on religious subjects. He took the name Fra Giovanni de Fiesole. In 1436 he was transferred to San Marco in Florence where he painted most of his murals, which were commissioned by the Medicis. Every day that he worked on this he would begin with a prayer. At the end of each day he would be weeping with emotion. Each monk's room was painted with scenes with angels and local landscapes. Savonarola was arrested here, in front of one of the paintings.

Painting, by an unknown artist, of the burning of Savonarola. It is thought to have been painted some time in the early 16th century.

In 1445 he went to Rome, to work on paintings for the Pope. He returned to Fiesole in 1450 as Prior of the monastery, but was recalled to Rome in 1453, when the Pope decided he needed more frescoes (wall paintings).

The name Fra Angelico was not given to him until after his death. Soon after his death, however, people began to call him this because he had been such a good, kindly and saintly man. Despite the fact that he moved among very worldly people in the course of his work he lost none of his simplicity, caring only for his painting and his religion.

Savonarola was popular among some of the poorer people. In his sermons he said that there should be fairer taxes and better treatment for the poor. He accused Pope Alexander VI of not acting like a man of God. Savonarola criticized him for cheating people out of their money by getting them to buy **indulgences** - pieces of paper which declared that your sins were forgiven and you could go to heaven.

Savonarola organized great fires in the middle of Florence, to which people brought their perfumes, paintings of beautiful women, chessboards and other 'luxuries' to be burned. His supporters raided houses and took away playing cards, dice, mirrors and musical instruments.

Pope Alexander VI was not prepared to put up with Savonarola's dangerous sermons, or with his support for Charles VIII. Alexander signed a document which **excommunicated** (expelled) Savonarola from the Church. Savonarola ignored the document and said that it was the Pope who was acting against God's law. Many people now became afraid to go to his sermons because they feared that the Pope might excommunicate them as well. In March 1498 some of Savonarola's enemies had him arrested and tortured. He confessed to 42 pages of 'crimes' and admitted that his prophecies had not come from God. Then, on 23 May 1498 Savonarola was hanged and his body was burned.

2.6 Machiavelli

What is the best way to run a country? What can a prince do to get the support of his people and hang on to power? Questions like these have been debated by people for thousands of years. This unit gives you some of the answers produced by a man who lived and worked in Florence at the beginning of the 16th century. See if you agree with **Machiavelli's** ideas.

The evidence is taken from two of Machiavelli's books, ***The Prince*** and ***Discourses on Livy***. Livy wrote about the early history of ancient Rome. The ideas of Roman writers, builders and artists were studied very carefully by people in the 15th and 16th centuries. Many people looked back with pride to the great days of the Roman Republic. Niccolò Machiavelli was one of them.

Machiavelli knew about government. After the Medici had fled from Florence, a republic was set up in their place. From 1498, Machiavelli served as a civil servant in this republic. In 1512 the republic failed and Machiavelli was imprisoned for a time. It has been said that *The Prince* may have been written to get Machiavelli back into favour once the republic had failed.

 SOURCE **A**

It is safer to be feared than to be loved. But a ruler must make himself feared in such a way that he does not become hated. If it is necessary to execute anyone, this should only be done if there is a proper and obvious reason. But above all he must not touch the property of others, because men forget sooner the killing of a father than the loss of their inheritance.

From 'The Prince', Chapter 17, written in 1514.

 B

History shows that if you set up a republic you should assume that all men are wicked, and are always ready to be vicious whenever they have the chance.

From 'Discourses on Livy', Chapter 3, written 1513–17.

 C

A prince should show that he can encourage those who have talents in the arts. He should reward those who improve in any way his city or his country. At suitable times of the year he should entertain the people with festivals or shows.

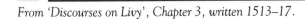

From 'The Prince', Chapter 21.

 D **SOURCE**

A conqueror, when seizing power, must decide about the injuries he needs to commit. He should get this done quickly, so that he will not have to keep harming people.

From 'The Prince', Chapter 8.

 E **SOURCE**

Everybody knows it is good for a ruler to keep his promises and not live by trickery. Yet experience has shown that the princes who have done great things are those who have known when to overlook their promises.

A prince must know when to act like a beast and when to act like a man. Men are wicked and do not keep their promises to you, so you do not have to keep your promises to them.

From 'The Prince', Chapter 18.

 F **SOURCE**

A ruler should not worry much about being plotted against if his subjects like him, but if his subjects are hostile and hate him, he should be afraid of everything and everyone. Once he has made his mind up he should not change it.

From 'The Prince', Chapter 19.

SOURCE G

A prince should have no other aim, and no other thought than war and its methods and practices. This is the only type of knowledge needed. It is so important because it keeps in power those who are born princes, but very often allows men of private status to become rulers. Princes who spend more on luxuries than weapons have often lost power.

From 'The Prince', Chapter 14.

SOURCE H

There is nothing that is so self-consuming as generosity; the more generous you are, the less you can continue to be generous. You will either become poor and despised or your efforts to avoid poverty will make you greedy and hated.

From 'The Prince', Chapter 16.

How should a prince stay in power?

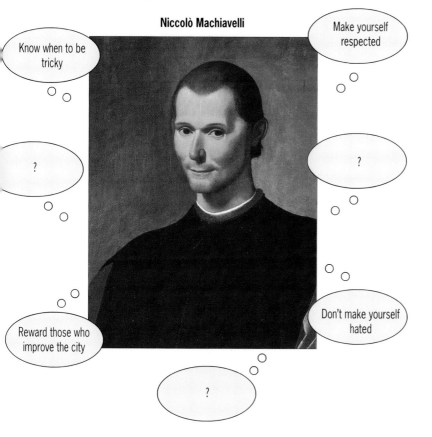

Niccolò Machiavelli

Know when to be tricky

Make yourself respected

?

?

Reward those who improve the city

Don't make yourself hated

?

Cesare Borgia

Cesare Borgia (1476–1507) was the son of Roderigo Borgia, Pope Alexander VI. His short, brutal and spectacular career earned him the admiration of many. Machiavelli is said to have based *The Prince*, a book about the ruthless manipulation of other people to get what you want, on Cesare.

When his father became Pope in 1492, Cesare was made Archbishop of Valencia. The next year he became a cardinal. Cesare was very tall with broad shoulders and a thin waist. He was immensely strong and had blazing blue eyes. He loved to show off. He was notorious for great cruelty and treachery and he was certainly responsible for many murders, including that of his brother-in-law, Alfonso.

In 1498 he gave up being a cardinal to marry the sister of the King of Navarre. In 1499 he became leader of the papal army, after he was suspected of murdering his brother, and led his army through central Italy, capturing town after town by bribery, trickery or terror.

When his father died in 1502 Cesare lost the protection that his father's position had given him. He also rapidly lost his power. His lands were taken from him and the new Pope, Julius II, had Cesare imprisoned in Spain. He escaped in 1506 but was killed the next year.

3.1 Perspective

Cartoon sketch for Leonardo's 'Adoration of the Magi', 1481.

Painting is just one example of the ways in which people can show how they think and feel about the world. If we look at paintings from different times we might be able to see whether some of those ideas changed or stayed the same.

To understand the changes which took place in painting during the Renaissance you need to know something about an idea called **perspective**. Sources A and B show you how a painting was planned. The painting is by Leonardo da Vinci. The planning sketch in Source A is called a **cartoon**. Many painters drew detailed cartoons before starting their paintings. The lines in Source A are called lines of perspective. Sources A and B are 'in perspective'. What do you think perspective is?

If you look carefully at Source A you should be able to find the **vanishing point** – the place where the lines of perspective seem to meet. Imagine you are looking down a railway track. At the place where you are standing the track seems very wide. As you look down the lines of the track get closer and closer until they seem to meet. That point is the vanishing point.

There are other paintings in the following units with carefully planned vanishing points. Why do you think the artists planned their paintings so carefully?

We don't know who 'invented' perspective. When we look at paintings from the Middle Ages we can see that many of them are not in perspective. Other things were more important to the artist than getting the perspective right.

In Florence in the early 15th century, there were a number of artists, map-makers, goldsmiths, mathematicians and scientists who knew each other and met to talk about new ideas. People learned from each other.

Filippo Brunelleschi was one of these clever people. He had read a book by the ancient Greek writer, Ptolemy. The book was called **Geography**. Not all the Greeks believed the world was flat. The book gave instructions about how you could use the laws of mathematics to work out what the world really looked like. Brunelleschi seems to have used Ptolemy's ideas in his work. Some writers have said it was Brunelleschi who should get the credit for telling the world about perspective.

Piero della Francesca

Piero della Francesca (1420–92) was a scientist and a mathematician as well as an artist. He had a mathematician's view of painting which he wrote about in a book, *On Perspective in Painting*. He worked in Florence, Rome, Urbino and Ferrara. He was a great painter but he preferred mathematics. He gave up painting during the last years of his life. His last book was about perfect proportion, called *On the Five Regular Bodies*.

B SOURCE

Leonardo's unfinished 'Adoration of the Magi', 1481.

3.2 Michelangelo

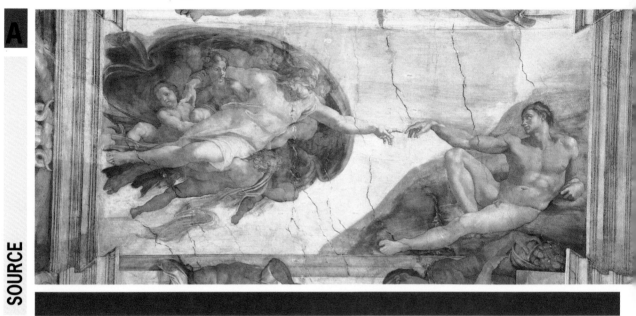

Detail of the ceiling of the Sistine Chapel, painted between 1508 and 1512.

What kind of a man locks himself away in a chapel and spends four years lying on his back, painting the ceiling? This was no ordinary chapel, and this was definitely no ordinary man. **Michelangelo** was born in 1475. His father allowed him to become an apprentice in a studio in Florence when he was 13. Soon Lorenzo de' Medici noticed his work and gave him a place at his school of architecture.

Lorenzo paid Michelangelo a wage and encouraged his study of sculpture. When Lorenzo died in 1492, Michelangelo had to look after himself. In 1496 he was given work in Rome by the Pope and won great praise for his sculptures. In 1501 he was called back to Florence by the government to make the famous statue of David which you can see in Unit 6.1.

In 1505 Pope Julius II called Michelangelo to Rome. Michelangelo spent a lot of effort, time and money choosing and buying marble for a tomb the Pope had asked him to build. When the Pope changed his mind in 1506 and decided he did not want the tomb, Michelangelo felt angry and let down. In March 1508 Michelangelo returned to Florence, but within two months the Pope summoned him back to Rome. This time he had to begin work on the painting of the **Sistine Chapel**. The Pope would not let him get on with the job he wanted to do – sculpture.

The idea of a genius whose ideas came from God, and who had superhuman powers only granted to a few rare people, can best be seen in the life and work of Michelangelo. It wasn't just his admirers who saw him in this light; he himself accepted that he was a genius, even though it was sometimes more of a curse than a blessing.

From 'The History of Art' by H. Janson, 1969.

Pope Julius II had the strength of will to inspire and bully. Without him, Michelangelo would not have painted the Sistine ceiling. For centuries, writers on Michelangelo have criticized the Pope for taking him off the work on the tomb, on which he had set his heart, and putting him to work on the Sistine ceiling. I think it was an act of inspiration. All writers on Michelangelo have given different interpretations.

From 'Civilization' by Kenneth Clark, 1969.

It is very difficult for any ordinary person to imagine how it could be possible for one human being to achieve what Michelangelo did in four years' lonely work in the chapel. He has given mankind quite a new idea of the power of genius. Each Pope seemed more keen than the last to obtain the services of the most famous artist of that time, and each Pope seemed more keen than the last to have his name linked with that of Michelangelo. He wrote 'I have served the Popes, but I only did this because I was forced to'.

From 'The Story of Art' by E.H. Gombrich, 1950.

Michelangelo worked on the ceiling of the Sistine Chapel from 1508 to 1512. When the scaffolds were taken down, people marvelled at his incredible work. The result astonished even the great painter Raphael.

Michelangelo had been tired out by four years of tough, lonely work. His neck was damaged by lying on his back for such a long time. His sight was so bad that he could only read a book if it was held above his head. The new Pope, Leo X, hired artists like Raphael but did not have any work for Michelangelo. So he went back to Florence and got involved in politics and warfare as well as art. Finally, in 1534, Pope Paul III asked Michelangelo to start work on another massive painting – this time on the huge wall at the entrance to the Sistine Chapel. The work was to take another five lonely years.

Michelangelo carried on working for another 30 years. The historian Vasari visited him when Michelangelo was 88 years old. He was a sad figure, hardly able to sleep. He worked by night and by day. He ate and drank very little. When death came it may have finally given him peace and rest.

Pope Julius II

Pope Julius II (1443–1513) was christened Giuliano della Rovere. He was sixty years old when he became Pope. He was proud of his lack of learning and liked to lead his armies in person. He wanted to free the papacy of foreign influence.

Julius was also a great patron of the arts. He employed Bramante to build St Peter's and his private rooms were decorated by Raphael. Michelangelo painted the frescoes on the ceiling of the Sistine Chapel for Julius, and designed Julius' tomb (although the work on this was never completed).

3.3 'The Last Supper'

We have seen how painters made very careful preparations before starting a painting. Now we will look at the way in which a cartoon sketch for a painting was planned. The painting is a famous one – Leonardo da Vinci's *The Last Supper*. It can be seen in Source A.

The painting was ordered in about 1495 by the powerful Duke of Milan. Leonardo was the Duke's court painter. The painting was to be done on a wall of a church in Milan.

At this time some artists used **fresco** painting. This meant that you painted straight on to a wall and had to work while the plaster was still wet (or 'fresh'). Leonardo's notebooks show that he made lots of careful sketches of the heads of the apostles before he started painting. We know something about the way in which Leonardo worked because a person who knew him described what he saw (Source B).

Leonardo worked for a long time on *The Last Supper*. The Duke of Milan wasn't very happy about all the delays. About two years after Leonardo had started the painting the Duke ordered his secretary to make sure Leonardo hurried up and finished it. The painting took at least three years to finish. Only 20 years after the painting had been finished people noticed that the wall had begun to rot.

'The Last Supper' by Leonardo da Vinci, painted 1495–8.

Perspective

The background of *The Last Supper* seems to be symmetrical – and also seems to 'go back into the wall'. This was done by the use of perspective. Can you see how the windows seem to disappear into the background?

Leonardo prepared his sketch for the painting in the following way. The sketch was divided in half to create a 'horizon'. The horizon was then divided in half to find the vanishing point, at the centre of the sketch. Two further vertical lines were then drawn to create a large square in the centre of the canvas, and diagonals from the centre to the corners of the square were drawn to form the lines of perspective. The large square was then further divided into smaller squares.

Christ was placed at the vanishing point, and then further groups of three people were placed on the sketch.

A

SOURCE

Many times I have seen Leonardo go to work early in the morning on the platform before *The Last Supper*, and he would stay there from sunrise until darkness, never laying down the brush but continuing to paint without eating or drinking. Then three or four days would pass in which he would spend hours examining the painting, but not touching it. Sometimes he would take a brush and give a few touches to one of the figures, and then he would leave and go somewhere else.

Description of Leonardo by his friend Matteo Bandello.

Raphael

Raphael (1483–1520) was one of the greatest painters of the Renaissance. He worked in many places, including Florence and Rome. His work combines the boldness of Michelangelo and the sweetness of Leonardo da Vinci. In 1514 he took over as architect of St Peter's.

3.4 Progress in Painting?

The changes brought about by perspective can be seen in Sources A and B. They are both about fighting and they both show battle scenes, but in very different ways.

Source A is obviously not in perspective. Does that mean it's not a 'good' picture? It was painted during the Middle Ages. Paintings and sculptures from the Middle Ages do not look very life-like, but they weren't supposed to be! The best way to make sense of art from this time is to ask what the artist or sculptor was trying to do or 'say'. Look at Source A and try to explain what this painter had to say about warfare in the Middle Ages.

Now look at Source B. It was painted by a man called **Paolo Uccello**, who spent hours and hours finding out about the 'new' ideas of perspective. People who knew Uccello said that he was so busy with his perspective drawings that when his wife told him it was time to go to bed he would hardly look up from his drawing. All he would say was: 'what a sweet thing perspective is!'.

13th-century painting showing knights in battle.

A

SOURCE

Look at the broken lances lying on the ground. Can you see the way in which they all seem to point towards the vanishing point? Can you find some more examples of perspective in this painting?

Uccello was said to have been most proud of the way he had painted the fallen soldier at the front left of the picture. It was said that no such figure had been painted before. What do you think is so unusual about it?

Source B is from a room in the Medici Palace in Florence, Italy. We know that the Medici were the richest and most powerful family in Florence in the middle of the 15th century. We also know that there was a battle at a place called San Romano in 1432, when soldiers from Florence beat their enemies. The Medici family were proud of winning the battle.

'The Battle of San Romano' by Paolo Uccello, painted in about 1450.

Boticelli

Boticelli (1445–1510) was christened Alessandro Filipepi and was taught to paint by Filippo Lippi. His most famous painting is The Birth of Venus which can be seen in the Uffizi Gallery in Florence. After the Pazzi plot (where the Pazzi family tried to assassinate two of the Medici family, but were caught by the people and hung) Botticelli was paid to paint pictures of the failed plotters with ropes around their necks. In 1482 he painted some of the frescoes in the Sistine Chapel in the Vatican in Rome. Botticelli became a follower of Savonarola. Though his style of painting was unfashionable by the time he died in 1510, it became popular again later. In Victorian times his paintings inspired the 'Pre-Raphaelite' and 'Art Nouveau' movements.

4.1 Changes in Building

The Colosseum, an arena built in Rome towards the end of the 1st century AD.

To understand change you need to know what existed before. In this unit we will be looking at buildings from different times. There were many changes in building styles from Roman times up to the Renaissance, but there is only space to mention a few of them here. It is also important to remember that these are the buildings of rich people or rich organizations. Evidence about the buildings of poorer people is harder to find.

Roman buildings

Sources A, B and C show Roman buildings. The Romans were very practical people. They conquered the Greeks and adopted some of their best ideas. Traces of aqueducts, roads and other buildings can be still be found throughout the huge area conquered by the Romans.

The Pantheon, a temple built in Rome in the 2nd century AD.

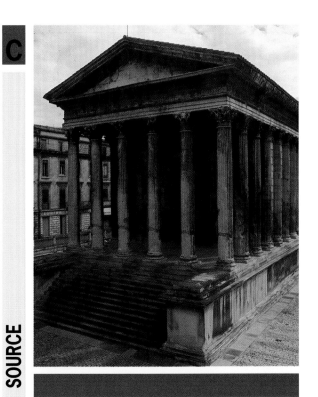

SOURCE C

The Maison Carrée, built by the Romans in Nîmes, France, in 16 BC.

SOURCE D

Milan Cathedral, Italy, begun in 1386.

Gothic buildings

Many new styles of building emerged in the thousand years following the fall of the Roman Empire. The buildings shown in Sources D, E and F come from this so-called **Gothic** period. Gothic is not a very helpful word to describe different styles of buildings from different places. It was used hundreds of years later by people who didn't much like the paintings, buildings and sculpture produced after the Romans and before the Renaissance. It was a term of abuse which has stuck.

Traders, travellers, kings and ambassadors all helped spread new ideas about building to different parts of Europe. French and German architects went to northern Italy to work on Milan Cathedral (Source D).

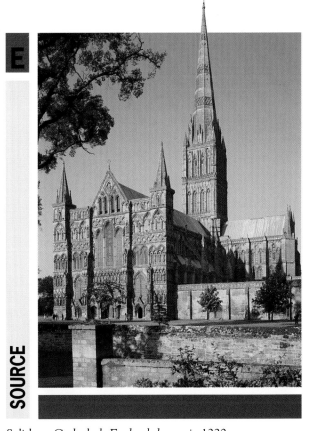

SOURCE E

Salisbury Cathedral, England, begun in 1220.

A painting of a mansion in France, 1413–16.

Renaissance buildings

Historical periods do not always start or finish at exact dates, so it's difficult to be certain when we can talk about the start of the changes known as the Renaissance. Sources G, H and I show buildings put up in the 15th and 16th centuries in Italy.

We have seen that the word Renaissance means the 'rebirth' of ancient ideas. Painting, sculpture and building are among the arts which are said to have been 'reborn'. The buildings shown in this unit give us clues about this 'rebirth'.

Hostel for orphans built by Brunelleschi in Florence, Italy, 1419–24.

Santa Maria Novella, a church in Florence, designed by Alberti and begun in 1458.

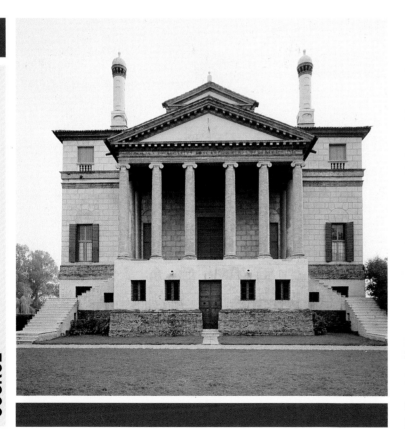

Alberti

Alberti (1404–72) was born in Genoa. His family were rich bankers. He was educated at Padua, so well that while still at school he wrote a play in Latin that became accepted as a 'genuine' Roman work. From 1428 he worked in Florence. He designed the church of Santa Maria Novella in pure classical style. After studying the work of Vitruvius, a Roman architect, he wrote *De Re Aedificatoria* which made people interested in old Roman architecture. He helped to design St Peter's in Rome. Alberti was also a musician, poet, athlete, painter and philosopher – a 'Renaissance man', brilliant in many ways.

Villa Malcontenta, designed by Palladio, 1560.

4.2 The Glory of Rome

Some of the 'Renaissance' changes in building took place in Italy in the early 15th century. Why did important changes take place in Italy rather than in other countries? What was so special about Rome? We can tackle these questions by finding out what the architects of the 15th century knew and thought about Rome.

SOURCE A

It is no surprise that these changes took place in Italy where a number of Roman buildings had survived. The climate made it easier to imitate these buildings in Italy than further north in Europe. Architects like Brunelleschi and Palladio went to Rome to study and measure these buildings and find out how they were built. There was also a book about building, written by the Roman architect Vitruvius, in which he wrote about the need for symmetry in architecture.

From 'The Renaissance' by Peter Burke, 1987.

SOURCE B

In the Forum, both public and private business is controlled by the town's officials. The site of the basilica should be fixed next to the Forum in as warm an area as possible so that in winter businessmen may meet there without being troubled by the weather.

From 'On Architecture' written by Vitruvius during the reign of the Roman Emperor Augustus. Vitruvius lived from 50 BC to AD 26.

Pope Nicholas V

Pope Nicholas V (1397–1455) was the Pope who brought peace to the Papal States (those lands in Italy ruled by the Pope). He set about restoring the glory of Rome. He began a new collection of books for the Vatican library. He collected old manuscripts and employed an army of copyists, translators, poets, historians and teachers.

Nicholas V asked the Florentine architects, Rossellino and Alberti, who loved classical Roman style, to plan churches, monasteries, palaces, piazzas and fortifications. They tore down ancient Roman temples and began to lay the foundations of a new St Peter's. When Nicholas died, the whole area that is now the Vatican City was covered in excavations for his planned new buildings.

'Ideal City', a painting by Piero della Francesca, about 1480. He was an artist who had worked in important centres of learning like Florence and Urbino. The round temple and wide open space fit in with ideas about town planning suggested by Alberti, the great Renaissance architect, painter and scientist. Alberti had made a careful study of the ruins of Roman towns.

SOURCE C

S.BIESTY

A modern reconstruction drawing of the Forum in ancient Rome. A religious procession has come past the temple of Julius Caesar (in the middle). The large building on the left is the basilica. It was used mostly as a law court and a meeting place.

4.3 The Incredible Dome

The dome of Florence Cathedral, built by Brunelleschi.

Filippo Brunelleschi (1377–1446) designed the dome of Florence Cathedral (Source A). Large domes were difficult to build because you had to find a way to stop them collapsing in the middle. Long planks of wood could be used to build small domes, but there just wasn't a tree big enough to build the dome for Florence Cathedral. If you look at Source B you can see that a huge amount of scaffolding needed to be built very high above the ground. Machines had to be powerful enough to raise very heavy stones to the top of the dome. These machines would need a source of power; men needed to work in safety.

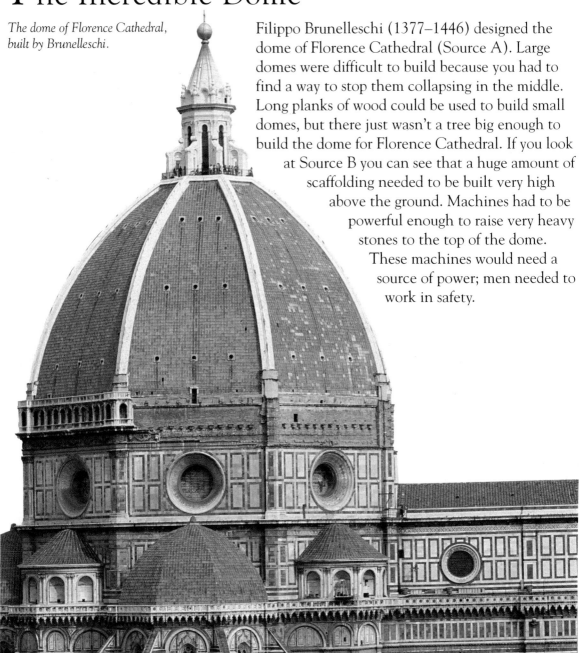

SOURCE

Ghiberti

Ghiberti (1378–1455) beat Brunelleschi in the competition to design doors for the Florence Baptistery. The job took most of the next twenty-two years. He also taught Donatello and Uccello.

Why was Brunelleschi able to build such a large dome? As you read the story of Brunelleschi, look for things which made it possible for this great dome to be built. Try to decide which of these things were more important.

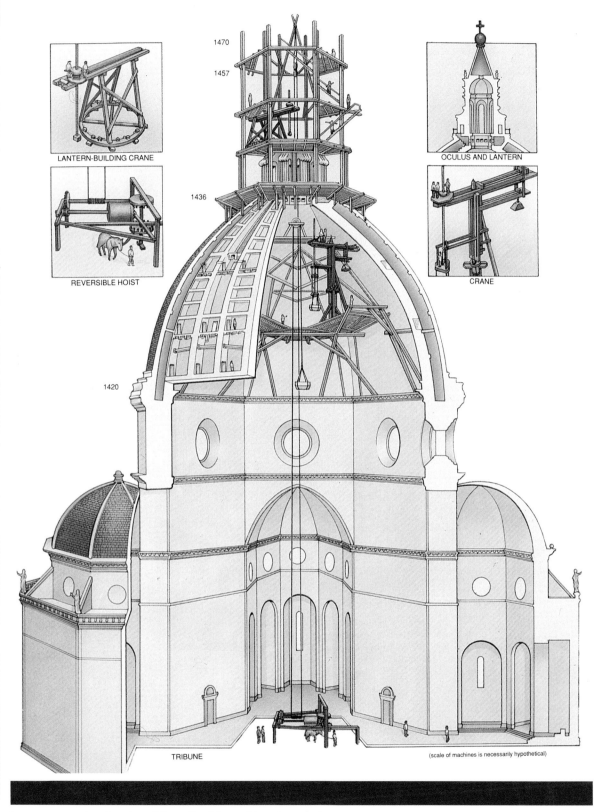

LANTERN-BUILDING CRANE

REVERSIBLE HOIST

OCULUS AND LANTERN

CRANE

1470

1457

1436

1420

TRIBUNE

(scale of machines is necessarily hypothetical)

A modern reconstruction drawing of Brunelleschi's machines in operation.

Who was Filippo Brunelleschi?

Brunelleschi had been a goldsmith before he became famous as an architect. He used his skills in working with gold to make his own sculptures from metals such as bronze. In 1401 there was a contest for sculptors. The prize was the important and valuable job of designing some special bronze doors at the Baptistery in Florence. Many good sculptors entered the contest. Brunelleschi's design was good enough to be placed second. Brunelleschi had wanted to win. It is said that he was so disappointed that he gave up sculpture and turned instead to designing buildings.

Brunelleschi went to Rome and made a very careful study of some of the great Roman buildings which were still standing. Pictures of some of these buildings can be seen in Unit 4.1. You can see what the inside of a famous Roman building looked like if you look at Source F on page 37.

When he returned to Florence, Brunelleschi studied the way in which large churches had been built in the Middle Ages. One of the problems in building large churches was in lifting large stones to great heights. From his studies of Roman and medieval buildings, Brunelleschi designed new scaffolding which made this possible.

According to legend Brunelleschi suggested that whoever could stand an egg on its head should be given the job of building the dome. He gently pressed an indent into the shell and it stood up. He got the job. He was also helped by the great scientist and astronomer Toscanelli, who taught him about mathematics.

Domes became more popular after Brunelleschi had shown that they could be built. St Paul's Cathedral, built in London by Christopher Wren, is just one example of a huge domed cathedral.

From 'Leonardo' by Ritchie Calder, 1970.

What man, however hard of heart or jealous, would not praise Pippo (Brunelleschi)? It is such a vast building, raised above the skies, that all the people of Tuscany could fit into its shadow. (Tuscany is an area of Italy around the city of Florence.)

From 'On Painting' by Leon Alberti, 1435. Alberti was a friend of Brunelleschi and was so impressed with his work that he dedicated his book to him.

From the Pantheon, Brunelleschi got the idea of building circles of stone. His own invention was to make the rings a mixture of bricks and stones. He then created an inner as well as an outer dome, to hold up the weight of this huge building. Brunelleschi designed machinery and ramps to haul up the stone, bricks and even wine for the workers to the top of the dome.

Building the dome of Florence Cathedral.

The Pantheon, a large round temple built in Rome in the 2nd century. It is still standing today. This picture was painted in about 1750 by Giovanni Paolo Pannini. The dome is 43.5 metres wide, and the 'eye' of the dome is the same distance above the ground. Do you think Brunelleschi might have copied some of the Romans' ideas?

Bramante

Bramante (1444–1514) was the architect who dominated the early Renaissance in Rome. He grew up near Urbino, became a painter, spent some time in Milan and went to Rome after the French captured Milan in 1499. Like Alberti, Bramante was devoted to the architectural style of the ancient Romans. His ideas appealed to Popes Alexander VI and Julius II in their creation of Renaissance Rome. The last fifteen years of Bramante's life were those when his best

work was done. He designed the new basilica of St Peter's and the foundation stone was laid in 1506. There were many arguments over the design. Bramante and Michelangelo became great enemies. When Bramante died Raphael took over the work on St Peter's. However it was Michelangelo who designed the great dome and he based it on Brunelleschi's dome in Florence. St Peter's was finally completed in 1626.

5.1 The Spread of Printing

Printing was an important development because it helped bring about other changes. In this unit we're going to look briefly at the story of printing in the hope that we might make sense of some of those changes. Before the time of printing, books in Europe were copied by hand (Source A). Monks did most of the writing. Therefore, most learning was controlled by the Church.

Printing did not begin in Europe. The Chinese knew about printing in approximately AD 500. They used **block printing** (see diagram). We don't know exactly how or when block printing arrived in Europe. We know that Arabs traded with the Chinese and knew about block printing. The Arabs found out about paper making after they captured Chinese paper makers in a battle in AD 751. Paper making spread all over the huge Arab Empire.

Many things were brought from China to Europe during the Middle Ages. Europeans found Chinese inventions, like **gunpowder**, very useful. People also seem to have been interested in block printing. This was partly because it helped to satisfy a craze for playing cards which swept through certain parts of Europe in the 14th century. The Church found block printing useful because it was able to produce lots of copies of pictures of saints or religious leaflets only a few pages long.

A medieval monk producing a book by hand.

A

SOURCE

Changes in printing.

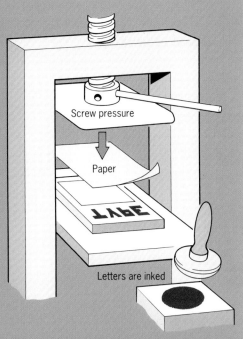

Screw pressure

Paper

Letters are inked

1 Block printing. Letters were carved in blocks of wood. These blocks were dabbed with ink and pressed on to sheets of paper.

3 A 15th-century printing press. The words were chosen for printing. The paper was placed on top of the inked letters and then pressed down. The same image could be produced many times.

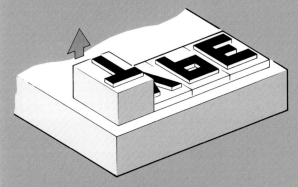

2 Movable type. Separate letters were made out of metal. They could be fitted in different combinations to make words.

A woodcut of a printing office in Nuremburg, by Abraham von Werat.

Movable type
The search was on for a way of printing whole books cheaply and quickly. In about 1436 a German merchant and goldsmith called **Johann Gutenberg** began experiments with printing presses in the town of Strasbourg. He spent much time and money before he found a way of printing with metal letters or 'types'. In 1454 Gutenberg produced some printing for the Pope. A new world had begun.

The spread of printing

If you look at the map you can see the rate at which printers' workshops were set up all over Europe. The first book to be printed with movable type is thought to have been the 'Gutenberg' Bible. Printing quickly spread to Italy. The Church was rich and there were many merchants and traders who wanted printed books and papers. Venice became an important centre for printing in Italy.

Changes

There was a huge **increase** in the number of books. This meant that more people learnt to read and write. It was now possible to learn at home rather than always having to go to an expert to get access to books. Many books sold large numbers of copies and reached a huge audience. There were new businesses which grew up around printing – for example, bookselling. There were new jobs in printing. These included the special skills of typesetting and proof reading. The skilled people no longer had to do the boring job of copying books by hand. They could be released to do other jobs which could help more people. All of this seems very good, but do you think there were any people who did not welcome the arrival of printing? Did it threaten any people's jobs or power?

Books were printed but so were all sorts of other things – such as pamphlets, adverts and newspapers. Printing also eventually helped create the jobs of journalist and novelist. Newspapers helped to give jobs to all sorts of other people. Before the age of printing there was great importance attached to memory. Storytellers had wandered from village to village. Histories and customs were sometimes passed on by word of mouth. What effect might printing have had on this?

Castiglione

Castiglione (1478–1529) wrote one of the most important books of the Renaissance, *The Book of the Courtier*. The book was about manners and behaviour. It was also about perfection. It gives us a wonderful insight into the Renaissance mind, illuminated by conversations that were supposed to have taken place in the palace of Urbino under the great Duke Federigo. The Duke sent Castiglione as an ambassador to England in 1506 where King Henry VII made him a knight. Castiglione was also an ambassador in Spain for Pope Clement VII.

SOURCE C

People used to think of printing as a key point in the history of civilization. Well, 5th-century Greece and early 15th-century Florence got on very well without it, and who shall say that they were less civilized than we are? Still, on balance I suppose printing has done more good than harm. Perhaps our doubts are due to what happened later.

From 'Civilization' by Kenneth Clark, 1969.

SOURCE D

There was an explosion of knowledge. New ideas spread more quickly, more people could read and more people took part in learning. But we must remember that there were still plenty of people who could not read, and there was still a lot of importance attached to pictures, for example, illustrated Bibles.

From 'The Printing Revolution in Early Modern Europe' by E. Eisenstein, 1983.

SOURCE E

As with most inventions, the ingredients were available; there was paper; artist's oil paint could easily be adapted for a suitable ink; prints were used in the textile trade. Books were already being printed by the use of wooden blocks; and block books continued to be used for a time.

From 'The Renaissance and Reformation' by J. New, 1977.

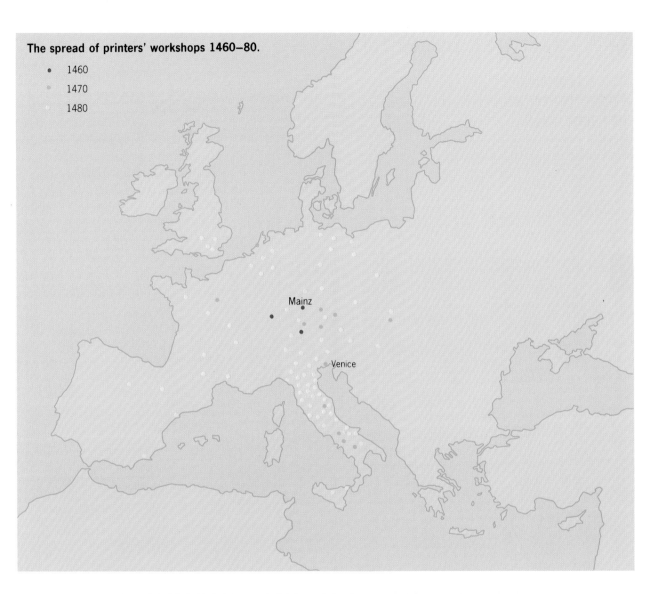

The spread of printers' workshops 1460–80.

- 1460
- 1470
- 1480

Mainz

Venice

Marguerite of Navarre

Marguerite of Navarre (1492–1549) was the sister of King Francis I of France. She married first the Duke of Alençon and then the King of Navarre. Her grandson became King Henry IV of France. At her court she encouraged thinkers and writers of all kinds. She was involved in the spread of ideas north from Italy. Marguerite corresponded with the great humanist philosopher Erasmus and was influenced by the writings of Martin Luther. She was a Catholic but believed in toleration, so gave her protection to Protestant reformers despite being accused of heresy by the Sorbonne.

Marguerite was a prolific writer. Her most famous work was the *Heptameron*, a collection of stories based on the theme of love that was modelled on the writing of the Italian, Boccaccio. She also wrote a long, mystical religious poem called The *Mirror of the Sinful Soul*. She also published a series of religious poems and hymns, some dramas and a non religious poem called *La Coche*. Her last works, published at the end of her life, show some mental anguish. In an age when women had few rights and were kept in the background of events, Marguerite was a shining beacon of intellectual achievement.

5.2 Changes in Warfare

How does change take place in history? Do changes just 'happen' or does one change lead to another? We can study these questions by looking at some of the changes which took place in **warfare** in Europe during the 15th century. Is there any sort of pattern to those changes or were they just accidents?

The bastioned trace, a system of defending castles or town walls from attack. It was also known as the 'trace Italienne' because the Italians played an important part in designing it. This idea was used in the building of walls in many different places in Europe after the introduction of gunpowder. The thick, squat walls and the slope of the bastion helped to prevent the damage that could be caused by cannon balls.

SOURCE

An important change in warfare came about with the introduction of **gunpowder**. There is evidence that the Chinese knew about gunpowder in the 9th century. The Chinese were the inventors of firearms. They had metal barrelled **cannon** in about 1250. These discoveries didn't spread quickly to Europe because for a long time there was little contact between China and Europe. Around the year 1350 we find that some Europeans were using firearms in battle.

In 1453 the Turks captured the important city of **Constantinople** from the Christians. They used gunpowder to destroy the walls of the city. If you look at the map on page 7 you can see that Constantinople lies in an important position. It is a sort of 'gateway' to Europe. Most of the continent was controlled by Christians at that time. From Constantinople, the Turks used their advanced miltary weapons to attack Europe. European cities and castles were defended by tall, thin walls at that time. The introduction of gunpowder brought new problems for people who were trying to defend their castles. Cannon balls did most damage when fired at the corners of a wall. If you look at Source A you can see how some Italians designed walls to make them stronger.

War was a costly business. It cost a lot of money to build the new **bastioned trace** walls. But once these walls had been built, it was possible to defend yourself against a very long siege. Big battles were very risky because a country could be beaten in an afternoon. Advanced defences meant that wars became longer and large numbers of men were needed to fight in them. There were other changes as well: more armies began to wear uniforms, instead of ordinary clothes. Can you think why this was so necessary? Also, gunpowder, cannon and small firearms were used more often in battle.

Francesco Sforza

Francesco Sforza (1401–66) was the illegitimate son of Muzio Sforza, a peasant who was a *condottiere* (a mercenary). The Italian Renaissance was a time when, as well as the arts flourishing, there was almost constant war. Much of the fighting was between rival city-states in Italy itself. So the Venetians fought the Milanese and so on. Many of the soldiers were *condottieri* and this made things very confused. They often changed sides, and even, if they had enough men on their side, tried to take over a city that they had been hired to protect!

This is what Francesco did. He was a good soldier, tough and aggressive. His stern discipline and concern for his men created a successful army. He also had the friendship of two powerful men, Cosimo de' Medici and Federigo, Duke of Urbino. Francesco was hired to help the Duke of Milan against the Venetians. He married the Duke's daughter but when the Duke died he left the city to the King of Naples. The Milanese did not want this and tried to set up a republic, with Francesco's army to defend it. However, Francesco besieged the city until they made him the Duke.

Size of Spanish, French and English armies, 1470–1630

	Spain	France	England
1470	20,000	40,000	25,000
1550	150,000	50,000	20,000
1590	200,000	80,000	30,000
1630	300,000	150,000	–

SOURCE

From 'The Military Revolution' by G. Parker, 1978.

5.3 Scientific Thought: Leonardo da Vinci

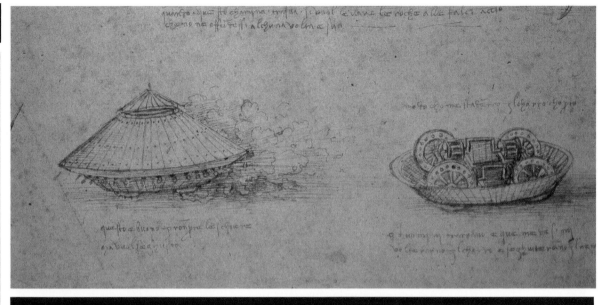

Source A shows a drawing of a very unusual machine. Have you any idea what it is? Sources A and B were drawn by Leonardo da Vinci. He was born in 1452. He lived in the city of Milan between 1482 and 1499, and between 1506 and 1511. Some of his most famous work, such as the painting of *The Last Supper* (see Unit 3.3) was done in Milan. Much of the rest of his life was spent in Florence.

Two sketches of a machine, from the notebooks of Leonardo da Vinci. It was a design which was never built.

We can discover many things about Leonardo from his own **notebooks**. The notebooks disappeared after Leonardo's death and were lost for hundreds of years. Since they were found, they have astonished everyone who has been lucky enough to read them. They contain beautiful sketches, like the foetus in the mother's womb (see Unit 1.1), and ideas for all sorts of inventions. If you look carefully at Sources A and B you can see some strange looking writing. Leonardo had his own special way of writing. It is a bit like a secret code. People were able to break the 'code' by reading the writing 'back to front' with a mirror.

A new way of thinking?
Science didn't begin during the Renaissance. The ancient Greeks produced a number of important scientists. They had ideas which were the result of careful **observation**. They wrote down their ideas carefully and in detail. Greek books were kept by the Romans and also by Islamic scholars.

In medieval Europe the Greek writers were often respected, but rarely challenged or improved on. Source D on page 46 gives an example of scientific learning in the Middle Ages. The Italian doctor is teaching his students about the body. He is reading from a Greek book about the body. His assistant is pointing to parts of the body, so that pupils can understand the book. The students were not encouraged to disagree with the book or to do their own scientific experiments. During the Renaissance, this changed. New scientific methods were being used and people were finding out more about their world.

In 1505 Leonardo da Vinci had a plan for a flying machine. If you look at Sources E and G you may get some idea of what that plan may have been like. The sketches in his notebooks also give us an idea of where he got some of his ideas from. They show very detailed pictures of birds in flight. His eye was so good that, centuries before cameras, Leonardo could draw the movements of birds' wings as if in 'freeze frame'. Leonardo also studied and sketched bats.

In producing his plan, Leonardo used the same methods as he had used when making his discoveries about the human body (see Unit 1.1). These methods could be called scientific observation. Leonardo observed, or looked at, birds and bats very carefully and made very detailed sketches of them from a number of angles. Leonardo loved birds and even released them from their cages, but he was prepared to dissect the dead bodies of these creatures as part of his scientific experiments.

Tycho Brahé

Tycho Brahé (1546–1601) had wanted to be an astronomer from when, as a child, he saw a partial eclipse of the sun. He was from a noble Danish family and had been well educated. He became the finest observer of the stars in the time before telescopes. His observations were very accurate and he measured the positions of seven hundred and seventy-seven stars. In 1572 he discovered a new star. Forced to leave Denmark, after travelling through Europe, he went to Prague and worked as an assistant to Johannes Kepler. He was a very hot tempered person and lost most of his nose in a duel when he was nineteen years old. He wore a false silver nose for the rest of his life.

Sketch of another machine from Leonardo's notebooks. This design was never built.

B

SOURCE

If you want to know about the parts of the body you must cut them up and examine them carefully from above, from below and from every side. Only in this way will you understand the body.

From the notebooks of Leonardo da Vinci.

If a man have a tent made of linen of which the openings have all been closed, and it be twelve braccia across and twelve in depth, he will be able to throw himself down from any great height without sustaining any injury.

From the notebooks of Leonardo da Vinci.

There are lots of 'doodles' and sketches of flying machines in Leonardo's notebooks. Some have one pair of wings, others two. Some have the pilot lying on a sort of surf board, others have him standing up. We are not told exactly what these are made of. At least one sketch shows a sort of helicopter. Leonardo had seen children's spinning tops. They date from the time of the ancient Chinese. Leonardo met lots of travellers at the house of his friend Toscanelli, the mathematician and astronomer. Maybe it was here that he saw a spinning top with a flying propellor on it. Leonardo had also studied an ancient Greek invention, the Archimedian Screw, which was used to raise water. He was fascinated by the idea of vertical lift. A model has been made of Leonardo's helicopter. It is powered by a tightly-wound spring. It was not until the 20th century that a working helicopter was finally built.

Woodcut from a book written in 1316 by the Italian doctor Mondino de Luzzi.

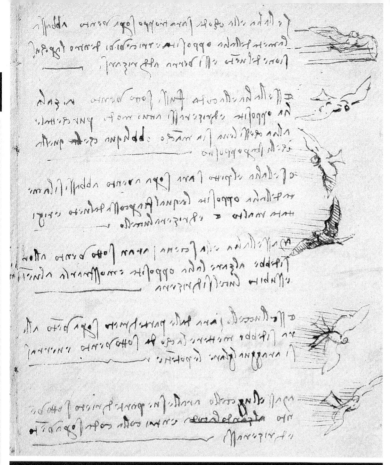

Leonardo's sketch of birds in flight.

Galileo

Galileo (1564–1642) was sent to Pisa University to study medicine, but was far more interested in science and mathematics. While professor of mathematics at Pisa University he made the famous experiment on velocity from the Leaning Tower of Pisa.

He moved to Padua in 1592. His observations of spots on the sun led him to support the idea that the earth revolved around the sun. This was not the accepted version of the way the universe worked. It was against the teachings of the Church, and so was seen as against God. He was forced to deny his ideas. He was imprisoned but later allowed to live in his own home.

Leonardo's plan for a flying machine. It had a rudder like a bird's tail, and was based on detailed observation of birds and flies.

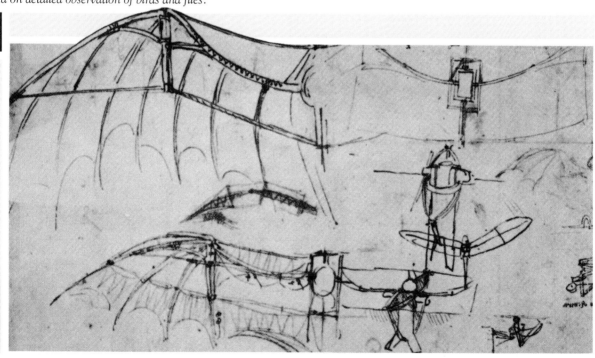

5.4 Alexander VI – Hero or Villain?

When we looked at the Italian city-states (Unit 2.1) we saw that the Pope had a lot of land and power in Italy. In this unit we are going to look at how a Pope used that power. We need to do this because the Popes played a part in bringing about the changes described in this book.

The Pope in question was **Alexander VI**. He was born Rodrigo Borgia in Spain in about 1430. He studied in Italy and went to the court of his uncle, Pope Calixtus III. Alexander was fat, bald, had a double chin and suffered from fainting fits. It was said that he became Pope by promising top jobs to people who voted for him. He chose the name Alexander in memory of the conquering Greek warrior, Alexander the Great. He called his son Cesare after the Roman dictator Julius Caesar.

You might find it strange that Alexander had a son, because Popes were expected to be unmarried, and not to have children.

Lutheran woodcut (1545) of Alexander VI; the lifted flap reveals a monster.

B SOURCE

He became Pope in 1492, the year in which Columbus opened up the **New World** by sailing westwards across the Atlantic Ocean to the islands we call the West Indies.

The Spaniards and Portuguese followed Columbus to the New World and began to conquer lands. They could not agree how to share out these new lands. The one person they could turn to was Alexander VI. He organized a deal between the two countries. A line was drawn across the world and each country agreed to stick to its 'half'. Of course the people in each 'half' of those lands were not asked what they thought about all this.

Alexander did everything he could to help his ambitious children. In 1499, Alexander allowed his son Cesare to build up his own state in central Italy. Much blood was shed (Source D). Alexander's death in 1503 helped put an end to his son's power.

Lucrezia Borgia

Lucrezia Borgia (1480–1519) was the daughter of Roderigo Borgia, Pope Alexander VI. Many stories were told at the time of her being involved in poisonings, murder and immorality, including sexual relations with her father and her brother, Cesare. It is based on gossip and rumour rather than evidence.

SOURCE C

The treasures of the Vatican Palace – paintings, sculpture, ancient manuscripts and rare books – cannot be compared. Yet in 1420 the Pope owned no more than about 300 books and hardly any great pictures or statues. To the Popes who ruled from 1471 to 1521 Rome owes a great deal of its present beauty. What a strange gallery these Popes make, yet they are as much creatures of the Renaissance as Michelangelo or Donatello. The strangest of all is Alexander VI.

From 'Rome: Splendour and the Papacy' by I. Origo, 1961.

Certainly her father used her to help his political plots – she had been married three times by the age of twenty-one. Her first husband, Giovanni Sforza, was divorced because her father fell out with his family. Her second husband was murdered by her brother. Her third husband was Alfonso d'Este, Duke of Ferrara. Lucrezia became very religious once she escaped her family. She encouraged artists, like Titian, and men of letters. She was only 39 when she died.

SOURCE D

Cesare Borgia continued his path of destruction. Joining forces with a new French army of invasion during 1501 he laid siege to the town of Capua in the name of his father the Pope. On 24 July he entered the town, which had been betrayed to him, and in cold blood massacred 5,000 of its inhabitants. It was probably the cruellest deed ever done in Italy, and every year on that day the bells have tolled.

Description of Cesare Borgia's siege of Capua, from 'The Florentine Renaissance' by V. Cronin, 1967.

5.5 Vesalius – Bodysnatcher

If you look carefully at Sources C and D you can see human skeletons. Compare them with the skeleton in Source A. What an amazing change in the way people understood the body! The man who brought about some of these changes was **Andreas Vesalius**.

What made these changes happen? Historians use the word **cause** to describe the things which make other things happen. Sometimes it is possible to find many causes for why something happened. Some causes might be more important than others. As you read the story of Andreas Vesalius, look for causes, or things which helped him find out more about the body.

The ideas of Claudius Galen

In 1533 Vesalius went to Paris to study with Jean Guinter, a man who had made a new translation of some of the books about the human body written by **Claudius Galen**. Thes were the best books about the human body available at that time. Galen was a Greek doctor who worked for the Romans. His ideas had been thought to be perfect for about 1500 years. If you look at Source B you can see how he worked. Can you see any problems in using this way of working to find out about the human body?

Skeleton from a 14th-century manuscript.

SOURCE

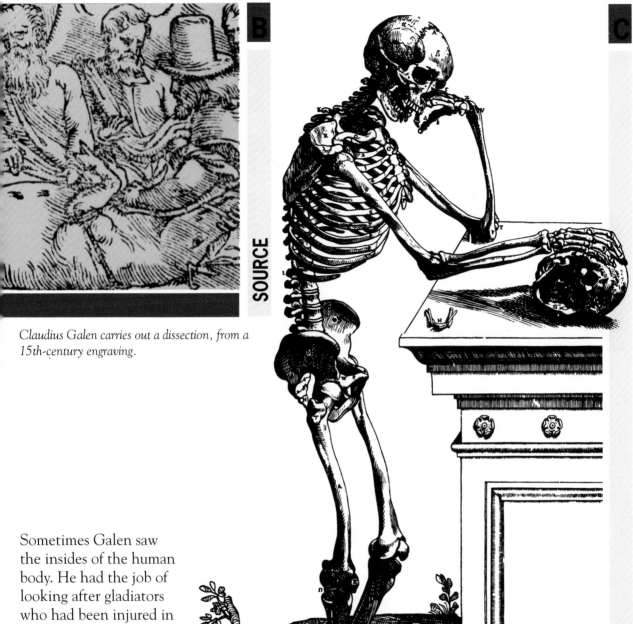

Claudius Galen carries out a dissection, from a 15th-century engraving.

Sometimes Galen saw the insides of the human body. He had the job of looking after gladiators who had been injured in fights with other gladiators, or with wild animals. Sometimes he could look into the body because bits of it were cut open – but this wasn't a very good way of learning about how it worked. For most of the time he had to carry out experiments on the bodies of pigs and apes.

SOURCE

This skeleton was drawn by Andreas Vesalius in the 1540s.

Andreas Vesalius

Andreas Vesalius was born in Brussels in 1514. His father was a doctor – maybe this was where his interest in medicine began. The young Andreas was so keen to find out about the body that he even stole the body of a criminal from the gallows, cut it up and examined it. Imagine the scene if you can; a young man chopping up a body, smuggling it back home in pieces and then starting the grisly job of putting the pieces back together again to make a skeleton.

When Vesalius went to Paris he was hoping to find out even more about the ideas of the great Galen. He felt that knowledge about **anatomy** (the parts of the body) had been lost since the time of Galen. Later on Vesalius explained what he was trying to do (see Source E).

Andreas Vesalius carries out a dissection, from the title page of 'Fabric of the Human Body', by Andreas Vesalius, 1543.

I wanted to find the lost knowledge about the human body. We may not be as perfect as the ancient teachers (men like Galen) but at least we can try to get near their standards.

From 'Fabric of the Human Body' by Andreas Vesalius, 1543.

The jaw of most animals is made up of two bones. In man, however, the lower jaw is made up of only one bone. Galen said that the jaw is not a single bone. Despite this I have not seen a jaw which is made up of two bones.

From 'Fabric of the Human Body' by Andreas Vesalius, 1543.

In 1537 Vesalius was made Professor of Anatomy at Padua University, Italy. This was one of the best universities in Europe. Padua was a very good place to learn about the body because the local law courts did not mind supplying the university with the dead bodies which were needed for dissection experiments. He did lots of **scientific experiments**. Most of them showed that the ideas of Galen were right.

However, sometimes Vesalius found that Galen had been wrong. This was a shock to him and to lots of people who believed in all of Galen's ideas. Yet each time Vesalius repeated his dissections he got the same result. Anyone who wanted to check his ideas could do the same experiments. The way Vesalius was working was new and different. Previously when the body didn't 'say' the same as the book, people said the body was wrong. It was the fault of the person who had cut up the body. Now Vesalius offered people a new **method** of working.

There were many good painters, sculptors and other artists in Italy at the time. Vesalius was lucky to be working at a time when important changes in art were taking place. If you look back at the pictures in Units 3.1–3.3 you can see how great those changes were. Sometimes artists turned up at an anatomy lecture and sketched what they saw. Vesalius knew that it would help his students if they had detailed pictures of the parts of the body to look at so he had pictures specially drawn.

Fabric of the Human Body
In 1543 Vesalius published a book which was like an atlas of the human body. The book was full of fantastic drawings. They showed the different layers of the body. Changes were taking place in the way in which books were made. Books could be printed and no longer had to be written out by hand. Many copies of the book could be made cheaply. You may be able to work out how this helped people like Vesalius. The book sold lots of copies and Vesalius became even more famous. He gave up working at the university and took a position as doctor to Emperor Charles V. Vesalius died in 1564.

Calcar

Calcar (1499–1546) was chiefly responsible for the illustrations in the famous book by Vesalius, *Fabric of the Human Body*. The book would not have made the impact that it did without the very detailed and accurate drawings of Vesalius' dissections.

As Jan van Stefan, from Calcar, he was a student of the artist Titian. He took the name of Calcar and became such a good student that expert judges sometimes mistook Calcar's paintings as Titian's. It was also said that he could imitate the style of Raphael so exactly that he could be mistaken for that artist too.

It is clear that Calcar was an excellent technical artist and that his skills were just what were needed for careful and detailed illustrations, such as Vesalius needed. These drawings are a tribute to Calcar's skill, and also to the rapid development of printing techniques, which allowed them to be so well reproduced. They were engraved onto metal plates which were carried over the Alps to Basle in Switzerland where they were printed. Some of the drawings were lost on the journey and had to be re-done!

Calcar had made an important contribution to a major scientific achievement. He died in Naples in 1546.

6.1 What was the Renaissance?

Before we can answer the questions when, where and why did the Renaissance take place, we need to know what the Renaissance was.

Renaissance is a French word and it means 'rebirth'. It can be a rather confusing word to use about the 15th century. The word 'Renaissance' is not thought to have been used by the people of the 15th century to describe the changes they were living through. The term was first used in a book written in 1855 by a French historian called Michelet, who used it to describe a whole period of time.

Another historian, Jacob Burckhardt, wrote a book called *Civilization of the Renaissance in Italy* and the word seems to have stuck ever since. Source A gives you an idea of the way in which an Italian writer of the 15th century saw the changes of that time.

A **SOURCE**

This century, like a golden age, has restored to light the arts, which almost disappeared; poetry, painting, sculpture, architecture and music. And all this in Florence. We are achieving what had been honoured amongst the ancient people, but which has been almost forgotten since then.

Letter by the Italian scholar Marsilio Ficino to Paul of Middelburg, 1492.

B **SOURCE**

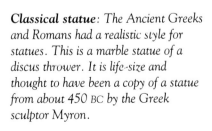

Classical statue: *The Ancient Greeks and Romans had a realistic style for statues. This is a marble statue of a discus thrower. It is life-size and thought to have been a copy of a statue from about 450 BC by the Greek sculptor Myron.*

SOURCE C

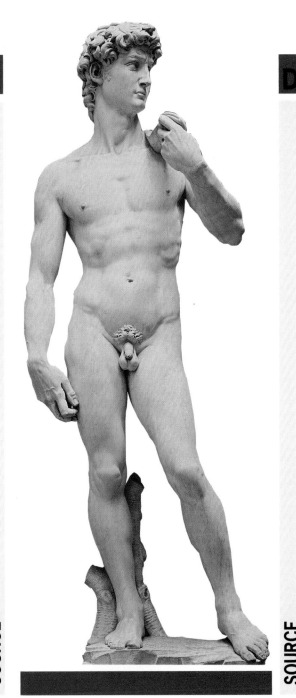

SOURCE D

Medieval statues: Religious statues from the west doors of Chartres Cathedral, France, about 1215.

Renaissance statue: 'David' by Michelangelo, 1501–4. It is 4m tall. Michelangelo is thought to have studied Greek and Roman statues like the one in Source B.

Giotto

Giotto (1266–1337) was called Giotto di Bondone. He was very influential on Renaissance art, breaking away from the stiff styles of previous artists.

In 1334 Giotto became Master of Works for Florence Cathedral. He designed the bell-tower, and decorated the front of the cathderal with statues.

6.2 When was the Renaissance?

Some events mentioned in this book.

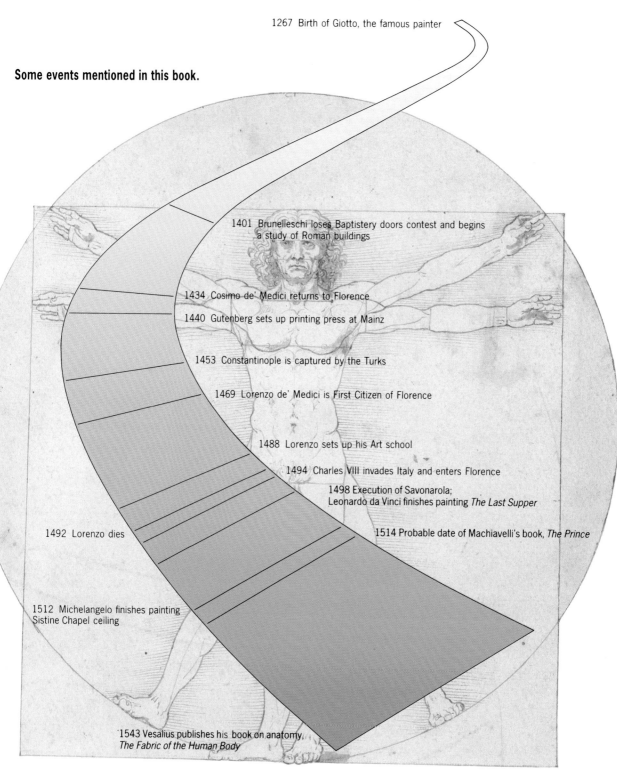

1267 Birth of Giotto, the famous painter

1401 Brunelleschi loses Baptistery doors contest and begins a study of Roman buildings

1434 Cosimo de' Medici returns to Florence

1440 Gutenberg sets up printing press at Mainz

1453 Constantinople is captured by the Turks

1469 Lorenzo de' Medici is First Citizen of Florence

1488 Lorenzo sets up his Art school

1494 Charles VIII invades Italy and enters Florence

1498 Execution of Savonarola; Leonardo da Vinci finishes painting *The Last Supper*

1492 Lorenzo dies

1514 Probable date of Machiavelli's book, *The Prince*

1512 Michelangelo finishes painting Sistine Chapel ceiling

1543 Vesalius publishes his book on anatomy, *The Fabric of the Human Body*

There is much debate about what the Renaissance actually was. The previous unit considered some of the changes in sculpture. A similar argument exists as to **when** the Renaissance happened.

Before we examine this question it's worth looking at the way in which historians divide up time. One way of dividing up time is to think of **units**, like years, decades, centuries. Another way is to think of **ages** like the Stone Age, the Bronze Age and the Iron Age. Periods of time like these don't always begin and end at definite, clear-cut moments.

When we ask about the timing of the Renaissance, we are not just playing a sort of guessing game. We are trying to be clear in our minds about the changes that took place, what they meant and how important they were. Some historians believe in the idea of **turning points** – the idea that some events were so important that things were very different afterwards. Some historians believe that the Renaissance was a turning point in the history of civilization. Other historians don't accept this idea.

SOURCE

I shall assume that the Renaissance means roughly the period between 1330 and 1530, though the economic picture would not change much if we added a few decades at the beginning or end.

From 'The Economy 1350–1500' by R. Lopez, 1953.

SOURCE

If by Renaissance we mean a period of time – broadly speaking the 15th and 16th centuries – then everything that happens within that time is Renaissance. However what we think of as the Renaissance style was not seen in many places until the end of this period.

From 'The Age of the Renaissance' edited by D. Hay, 1986.

Cellini

Cellini (1500–71) was a brilliant artist and goldsmith. He was also a terrible liar and braggart. Cellini wrote an amazing autobiography, which is full of exaggeration and self praise, and which gives an exciting picture of the people and the times of the Renaissance.

Cellini was born in Florence but was banished from the city because of a duel and went to Rome. His craftsmanship earned him the custom of nobles and high churchmen. Even the Pope asked him to work for him. But while his work was excellent and in great demand, his temper and unscrupulous nature were always getting him into trouble. He claims to have been an expert with sword and dagger and certainly he spent a lot of time in prison or being thrown out of cities for fights where his opponents were killed or maimed. He also spent time in prison for embezzling money.

In 1537 Cellini went for a short visit to France and was received by King Francis I. It was here that Cellini made the gold salt cellar that is a fine example of his work.

Cellini then returned to Florence and worked for Duke Cosimo I, where he created the famous bronze statue of Perseus with the head of Medusa. But he was in and out of trouble until the end of his days.

6.3 Where was the Renaissance?

Many of the changes described in this book took place in Florence and Rome, but these were not the only cities of the Renaissance.

Frederigo, the first Duke of **Urbino** (in Italy), ruled from 1444 to 1482. He was a great soldier who had fought his way to fame and fortune. He built a great palace and had a huge library (Source A). Rich men from far away sent their sons to be educated at Urbino. Paolo Uccello (Unit 3.4) and Piero della Francesca (Unit 4.2) both worked at Urbino. Sculptors, architects and scholars all came to this great centre of learning.

Leonella, Duke of **Ferrara**, ruled from 1441 to 1450. He employed a teacher from Urbino and made his court a great centre for poetry and drama.

Universities played an important part in the Renaissance. Some of the greatest thinkers and scientists had an international education. **Nicolaus Copernicus** (1473–1543), for example, is famous as the person who announced that it is the earth which goes around the sun, and not the sun which goes around the earth. One of the reasons why Copernicus was able to make this discovery was that he had received a very good education. He studied at universities as far apart as Cracow, Bologna, Padua and Ferrara. He also taught mathematics at Rome University. We have seen that Vesalius studied at Paris and Padua (Unit 5.5). **William Harvey**, who made discoveries about the circulation of the blood, studied at Cambridge University and then between 1599 and 1602 went to Padua. The fame of this university had spread far and wide.

A reconstruction of the anatomy theatre at Padua University, Italy. Large numbers of students could watch as their teacher dissected the dead body which had been brought in and placed on the table in the middle of the theatre. This was a very different way of learning from the old method of listening to the teacher read from a book.

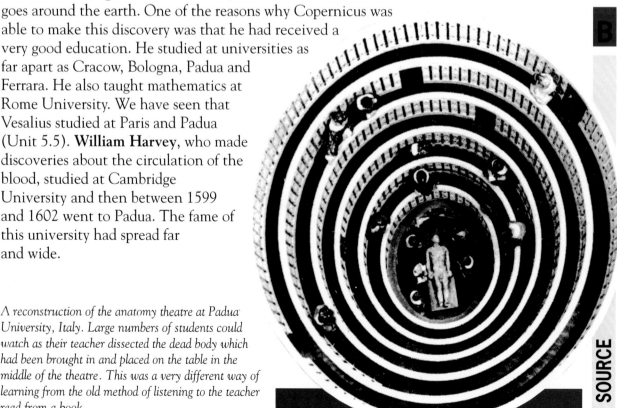

Francis I was an important patron of the Renaissance in **France**. He had spent time in Italy and was very impressed with Italian civilization. He wanted his court to be even more magnificent than those he had seen in Italy. He tried to bring the great Italian goldsmith Cellini to France, and promised 'I will choke you with gold'. He was the first king outside Italy to build up a large collection of Italian paintings and sculpture. He persuaded Leonardo to come to France and live his last years at Amboise. Francis's sister, Marguerite of Navarre, encouraged artists and writers to come to her court. She was a friend and patron of the great French writer, Rabelais.

The Renaissance in **Venice** didn't develop in the same way as it had done in Florence. Venice became a very important centre for musicians. Perhaps the greatest of these musicians was Claudio Monteverdi, who came to Venice from Mantua in 1611. The quality of his music encouraged others to follow his example. We have seen that Venice was a very important centre of trade. New ideas flowed along these trade routes. Oil painting became more important in Venice than in other cities. One of the reasons for this was the fact that traders from Venice were in contact with the trading cities of Bruges and Ghent – where some of the best oil painters worked.

The Chateau of Chambord, France, begun 1519 and built for the French King Francis I. It was originally a hunting lodge. Francis I ordered an Italian architect to redesign it. For 12 years 1,800 workmen worked to complete it.

The discovery of the individual was made in early 15th-century Florence. Nothing can alter that fact. But in the last quarter of the century the Renaissance owed almost as much to the small courts of northern Italy – Ferrara, Mantua and, above all, Urbino. The court of Urbino under Frederigo was a high point in the history of civilization.

From 'Civilization' by Kenneth Clark, 1969.

The map showing the spread of printing workshops (Unit 5.1) shows that Venice was one of the first places which received this new technology. Gutenberg had worked in Strasbourg and Mainz. Soon his work was being adapted not only in Venice but also in other parts of Europe, by people like William Caxton. In 1477 Caxton began printing books in England. He had travelled in Europe and had seen one of the new printing presses. Caxton's printed books helped the spread of new ideas from Europe.

Jan van Eyck was born in about 1385. Jan and his brother Hubert worked as artists in Ghent and Bruges. The brothers may not have invented oil painting, but they helped to make it more popular. Before oil painting, artists had mixed their colours either with water (for frescoes) or with egg yolks (tempera painting).

According to legend, Jan finished painting a panel, varnished it and put it out to dry. When the panel cracked he is said to have been so angry that he decided to find a better way. He experimented with oils and found that they dried quickly and kept the colour bright, even in the damp climate of northern Europe. Fresco painting made sense in the hotter climate of a place like Florence, but not in the chilly Netherlands.

Renaissance style architecture became very popular in England. It became part of the education of rich people in the 18th century to learn more about the Renaissance. They would travel to Europe on a **Grand Tour** of Rome and other great cities. They would see the ruins of ancient Roman buildings and find out about the new ideas of the Renaissance. The 18th-century writer Dr Johnson said that a man who had not been to Italy was always aware of being inferior.

'Giovanni Arnolfini and his bride', an oil painting by Jan van Eyck, 1434. Giovanni was an Italian businessman. The young couple are getting married. The words above the mirror say 'Jan van Eyck was here'; the artist was a witness at the wedding and he is one of the figures reflected in the mirror. Van Eyck had visited Italy and probably saw the work of some of the great Italian painters.

SOURCE

A Renaissance style building in England. St Paul's Cathedral in London was designed by Sir Christopher Wren, and built between 1675 and 1710.

Erasmus

Erasmus (1466–1536) was a Dutch Humanist scholar, whose books include:

Date:	1500	1505	1511
Book:	*Adages*	*Enchiridion*	*In Praise of Folly*

As well as writing his own books, Erasmus translated the works of early Christian writers and Greek scholars. He also produced, in 1516, an early version of the *New Testament* in Latin, called *Novum Instrumentum*, which set scholars all over the Christian world trying to write their version.

Erasmus became a priest in 1492, joining the priesthood from a monastery near Gouda. He found the new humanist ideas, that were spreading from Italy, fitted what he believed. So he went to Paris to study and teach these ideas. He then taught in many of the great centres of learning, including Oxford and Cambridge, spreading humanist ideas all over Europe.

Erasmus was in favour of reforming the Catholic Church and criticized the faults and abuses that he saw going on inside it. However, he also criticized Protestants, such as Martin Luther, who were trying to force reforms. He felt that, by demanding the replacement of the Catholic Church with another church, they were throwing out much of what was good in the Catholic Church, as well as what was bad. He felt gradual reform was most likely to take hold, while violent reform was likely to be rejected.

6.4 Why was there a Renaissance?

This book has described some of the changes which took place during the Italian Renaissance. We saw in the last unit that the Renaissance wasn't limited just to one country – it happened in many places. So if we look at the Renaissance as a whole, why did these changes take place? What sorts of causes can we find?

The unit on city-states (Unit 2.1) made the point that important **political changes** were taking place in Europe in the 15th century. Countries like France were emerging from damaging civil wars. Some rulers and nobles were becoming rich and powerful enough to become important **patrons**. The Duc de Berry, for example, never became King of France, but he was important and rich enough to have many artists and craftsmen working for him. Ambassadors **travelled** between the leading courts of Europe and sometimes brought fresh ideas and fashions with them. The oil painter, Jan van Eyck, is known to have visited Italy and may have taken important ideas back to Holland with him. When we looked at the way in which parts of Italy were governed we saw that city-states were sometimes good places for artists to work.

The trade map on page 7 shows that there were important international **trading routes**. Cities like Venice and Florence grew in size and importance and benefited from this trade. Bankers, industrialists and merchants were some of the people who became patrons of the arts. One of the reasons why new techniques in oil painting reached Venice before other Italian cities was that Venice had such good trading contacts with the Netherlands, the home of some of the best oil painters. Trade brought new technology from the advanced Islamic and Chinese civilizations.

Latin continued to be the language of the Church in the Renaissance, as it had been throughout the Middle Ages. Latin was also the language used by most scholars who were trying to reach an international audience. The scholar Erasmus, for example, only wrote in Latin. University lectures were given in Latin. In the 15th and 16th centuries the **importance of other languages** was also recognized. Writers like Machiavelli and Guicciardini wrote in their own language, Italian, as well as in Latin. This helped their work to reach more people. Some of these people attended the new universities which were being set up in a number of different European countries.

Federigo da Montefeltro

Federigo de Montefeltro (1444–82) wa educated in Mantua. His teacher, Vitto da Feltra, was famous and Federigo seems to have agreed that he was a g teacher. He said, later, that he had be instructed 'in all human excellence'.

Federigo was then sent off to learn the skills of war. As the Italian city-states spent much of their time fighting each other, the normal occupation of the tir was as a *condottiere*, a mercenary. Federigo seems to have been a successful student of war. As a militar leader he was a great general, never cruel, kind to the defeated and also considerate to his troops. It was said he never lost a battle, even when outnumbered. He was one of the few *condottieri* who was trusted by his employers. Because he was so successful, Federigo made lots of mo

In 1443 Federigo's brother, Oddanton became ruler of Urbino. At that time Urbino was little heard of, full of the us jostling for power. Within a year Oddantonio was assassinated.

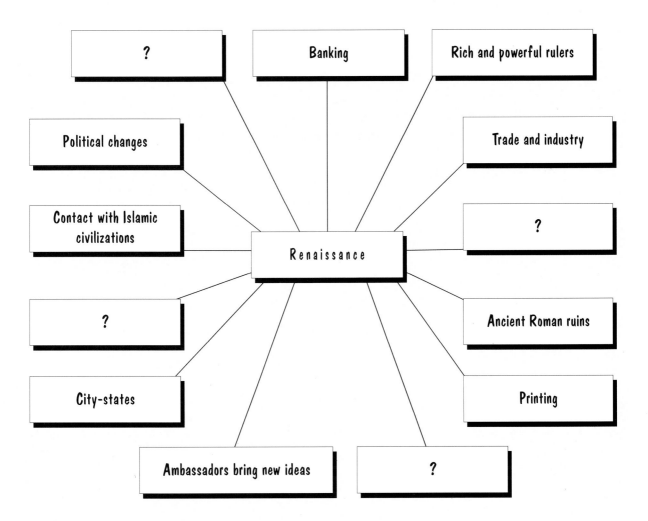

A concept map with "Renaissance" at the centre, connected to boxes labelled: ?, Banking, Rich and powerful rulers, Political changes, Trade and industry, Contact with Islamic civilizations, ?, ?, Ancient Roman ruins, City-states, Printing, Ambassadors bring new ideas, ?

derigo became ruler of Urbino. He
pt up his mercenary work, and so he
pt on making money. This meant he
uld keep taxes low, which made him
pular, and settled the city down. He
en spent a great deal on his court.
bino became a place where rich
nilies sent children to be educated.
omen were respected and played an
tive part in the court. He was
scribed as 'the light of Italy' by
stiglione. He was a typical
naissance combination: a man of
ture, violence, learning and politics.

The power of the Pope and of the **Roman Catholic Church** was very great in Renaissance Europe. The Church was an extremely important patron. All sorts of artists and craftsmen improved their skills while working on religious buildings. Many Renaissance paintings and sculptures are about religious subjects. Brunelleschi's new ideas about engineering and technology were used in building the cathedral in Florence (Unit 4.3).

New **technology** such as the development of the printing press (Unit 5.1) produced many different changes. People in a number of European countries could now afford the new books of men like Vesalius. These books could be translated into different languages.